MW00586044

Charts

Easy Excel Essentials
Volume 3

M.L. HUMPHREY

Copyright © 2017-2018 M.L. Humphrey

All rights reserved.

ISBN: 978-1-950902-32-3

Also published under ISBN 978-1720562832

TITLES BY M.L. HUMPHREY

EASY EXCEL ESSENTIALS
Pivot Tables
Conditional Formatting
Charts
The IF Functions
Formatting
Printing

EXCEL ESSENTIALS
Excel for Beginners
Intermediate Excel
50 Useful Excel Functions
50 More Excel Functions

EXCEL ESSENTIALS QUIZ BOOKS
The Excel for Beginners Quiz Book
The Intermediate Excel Quiz Book
The 50 Useful Excel Functions Quiz Book
The 50 More Excel Functions Quiz Book

DATA PRINCIPLES
Data Principles for Beginners

BUDGETING FOR BEGINNERS
Budgeting for Beginners
Excel for Budgeting

WORD ESSENTIALS
Word for Beginners
Intermediate Word

MAIL MERGE
Mail Merge for Beginners

POWERPOINT ESSENTIALS
PowerPoint for Beginners

CONTENTS

INTRODUCTION

In *Excel for Beginners* I covered the basics of working in Excel, including how to format in Excel and how to print. In *Intermediate Excel* I covered a number of intermediate-level topics such as pivot tables, charts, and conditional formatting. And in *50 Useful Excel Functions* I covered fifty of the most useful functions you can use in Excel.

But I realize that some users will just want to know about a specific topic and not buy a guide that covers a variety of other topics that aren't of interest to them.

So this series of guides is meant to address that need. Each guide in the series covers one specific topic such as pivot tables, conditional formatting, or charts.

I'm going to assume in these guides that you have a basic understanding of how to navigate Excel, although each guide does include an Appendix with a brief discussion of basic terminology to make sure that we're on the same page.

The guides are written using Excel 2013, which should be similar enough for most users of Excel to follow, but anyone using a version of Excel prior to Excel 2007 probably won't be able to use them effectively.

Also, keep in mind that the content in these guides is drawn from *Excel for Beginners, Intermediate Excel,* and/or *50 Useful Excel Functions*, so if you think you'll end up buying more than one or two of these guides you're probably better off just buying *Excel for Beginners, Intermediate Excel,* and/or *50 Useful Excel Functions*.

With that said, let's talk Charts.

CHARTS – TYPES

Charts are a great way to visualize your data. There's nothing like a nice bar chart or pie chart to see exactly what's going on. You know what they say, a picture's worth a thousand words. And seeing one big chunk of color dominating all the others tells you everything you need to know about who your best customer is or what your biggest expense is.

Just like with pivot tables, your data needs to be arranged properly before you can use charts. Specifically, for most of the charts we're going to discuss, you need one set of labels across the top and one set down the side with values listed in the cells where those two intersect.

Here are two examples:

Data Table Option 1

	Amazon	Createspace	ACX	Con Sales
201701	$100.00	$37.00	$23.50	$10.00
201702	$107.00	$39.59	$25.15	
201703	$114.49	$42.36	$26.91	
201704	$122.50	$45.33	$28.79	$25.00
201705	$131.08	$48.50	$30.80	
201706	$140.26	$51.89	$32.96	$8.00

Data Table Option 2

	201701	201702	201703	201704	201705	201706
Amazon	$100.00	$107.00	$114.49	$122.50	$131.08	$140.26
Createspace	$37.00	$39.59	$42.36	$45.33	$48.50	$51.89
ACX	$23.50	$25.15	$26.91	$28.79	$30.80	$32.96
Con Sales	$10.00			$25.00		$8.00

This is fictitious sales data for each month for various sales platforms. In the first example, the sales channels are listed across the top and the months are listed along the side with the intersection of those two showing the dollar value of sales for that sales channel for that period.

In the second example, each month is listed across the top and each of the sales channels is listed down the side.

(My version of Excel will work with your data in either configuration, but I'm pretty sure that's not how it used to be.)

To create a chart from your data, highlight the cells that contain your labels and values. In the examples above that would either be G1:K7 or M1:S5.

(Do not include any summary rows or columns.)

After you've selected your data, go to the Insert tab and click on the Chart type you want.

As you hold your mouse over each chart selection you'll see a version of the chart appear, but the chart will not be inserted into your worksheet until you click on an option.

We'll discuss each chart type in detail next, but the general rule is that for time series data like the examples above that include multiple variables (your sales channels) across multiple time periods (each month), the best choices are column charts, bar charts, and line charts.

For data where you have multiple variables but no time component, a better choice is a pie or doughnut chart.

Scatter charts are good for random data points where you're looking at the intersection of two or three variables to see if there's any sort of relationship between them.

(Excel does offer additional chart types like bubble charts and radar charts, but we're not going to cover them in this guide.)

Now let's walk through each chart type (column, bar, line, pie, doughnut, and scatter) in more detail:

Column Charts

The top-left chart option in the Charts section of the

Insert tab is Column Charts. It's the image with the upright bars.

There are seven possible column charts that you can choose from, but I'm going to focus on the top set of choices, which are the 2-D versions, since most of the 3-D versions are the exact same except three-dimensional.

For 2-D, you can choose from clustered columns, stacked columns, and 100% stacked columns. Here is an example of all three using the exact same data:

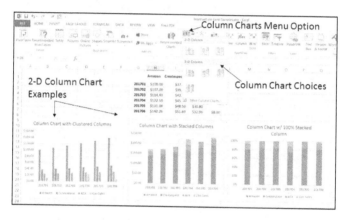

The difference between the clustered columns and the stacked columns is that the clustered columns version puts the results for each variable side-by-side for each time period. You can easily see the height difference between different results, but it can quickly become too busy if you're dealing with a large number of variables. For example, I have nine sales channels I track. Having nine columns side-by-side for each of twelve months would be overwhelming.

For my situation the stacked columns option is a better choice. Like with clustered columns, stacked columns have different column heights for each variable based on their value, but the columns are stacked one atop the other instead of shown side-by-side for a time period.

This means you end up with only one column per time period separated into colored sections that represent the relative size of each of the inputs.

The stacked columns option lets you see the overall change from time period to time period based on the total height of the column. You can also sometimes see the change for an individual input over time if the change is significant enough.

The 100% stacked columns option presents all of the information in one column just like stacked columns does, but instead of basing each section's height on that input's value, it shows that input's percentage share of the whole.

While you lose any measurement of value (a column chart with values of 2, 5, and 5 will look the exact same as one with values of 20, 50, and 50 or 200, 500, and 500), you can better see changes in percent share for each input. (A variable that goes from 10% share to 50% share will be clearly visible with 100% stacked columns.)

Which graph you choose will depend on what your goal is in performing your analysis.

My preference is for the stacked columns option. It lets me see the overall trend in the total while still allowing me to see significant changes in individual share of the whole and without overwhelming me with too much data in too small a space.

My second choice would generally be the clustered columns option although, as I mentioned above, it can look cluttered when there are too many inputs and it doesn't show the overall trend as well as the stacked columns chart does.

I personally don't like the 100% stacked columns option. As I mentioned above, it hides changes in absolute value. So you could go from making $10,000 to $100 and as long as the relative share for each input remained the same you wouldn't see that change in your graph. It's really only good for when you want to monitor relative change in individual components over time.

Bar Charts

Bar charts are the next chart type you see under the Charts section of the Insert tab. They're just like the column charts, except on their side.

They too have a clustered, stacked, and 100% stacked option available in both two-dimensional and three-dimensional versions.

Here are examples of the 2-D versions:

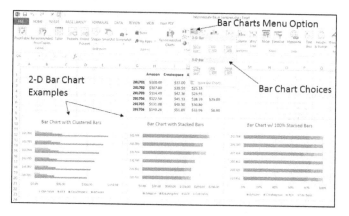

The pros and cons for each chart type are the exact same as for the column charts and if I were to use them instead of using a column chart (my preference), I would generally use the stacked bars option.

Line Charts

Line charts are the first chart type shown in the second row of choices. There are seven options listed, but you should only use the first choice on the left for each of the 2-D rows of choices.

This is because the other four 2-D options really aren't viable for a line graph. They're meant to do what the stacked columns graphs do and show relative values, but people just don't read line graphs that way. You expect that if there's a line drawn on a graph that it's showing actual values for that particular variable not relative values or cumulative values

The 3-D option is a more advanced chart type that creates an actual three-variable line graph. You can also use it to create a two-variable line graph with a three-dimensional line, but don't. (Remember, keep it simple.)

Here are examples of the basic line chart and the line chart with markers:

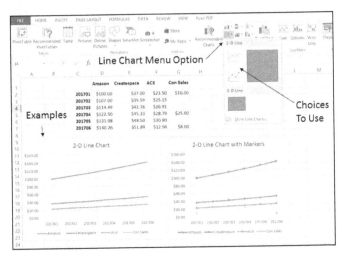

As you can see, they're basically the same except that one has dots along the line to show each data point and the other presents a smooth line. These graphs both chart actual values for each input. You can clearly see on both that the blue value (Amazon) dominates the other values in the chart.

Also note that the 2-D line chart of Con Sales, which doesn't have values for each period, is missing but that the 2-D Line Chart with Markers at least shows the data points. So if you have data that does not have values for each period you should use the line chart with markers option.

(If you replace those blank values with 0 instead, then Excel will draw a line on both charts and that line will show zero values for the blank periods. Another option is to replace the blanks with =NA() but in that case Excel just draws a line between the available data points and it looks on the graph like there weren't zero-value periods in the data.)

Pie and Doughnut Charts

Next we have pie and doughnut charts. These are best used when you have a set of variables that cover one period of time. So I've built the below examples using just the total values for each of the sales channels.

(To select a subset of your data, like I've done here, you can use Ctrl and your mouse to highlight just the sections you want before you choose your chart type. Or you can select all of the data, choose your chart type, and then go to Select Data and remove the data you don't want to use.)

There are three two-dimensional pie chart options and one doughnut chart option. The three-dimensional pie chart option is the same as the basic pie chart except in three-dimensions.

Here are examples of the two-dimensional pie charts and the doughnut chart:

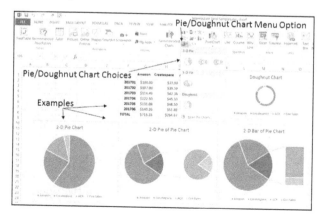

For the pie charts, you can choose between a standard pie chart, a pie of pie chart, or a bar of pie chart. As you can see, the doughnut chart is just like the basic pie chart except it's just the perimeter ring. It's like if you hollowed out the pie chart and just left the "crust".

If you're only focused on who or what accounts for the biggest share, then use the standard pie chart or the doughnut chart options.

If you want to be able to clearly see the results for all of your segments, even the smallest ones, then the pie of pie chart or the bar of pie chart are potentially better choices.

Both the pie of pie chart and the bar of pie chart combine the smallest entries into one single slice in the main pie chart. They then take those small entries and break them out into a separate chart.

For the pie of pie chart this second chart is another pie chart. For the bar of pie chart this second chart is a bar chart.

So, for example, in the sample we're seeing here, ACX and Con Sales were combined in the main pie chart and were then broken out in the secondary chart

In the main chart together they represent 18% of the total. In the right-hand chart they represent 78% and 22% *of that 18%.*

(To make it even more confusing, if you were to insert labels on the secondary charts, the labels would be the share that each one had of the overall whole, so the smaller charts would show 14% and 4% as the labels.)

I think this is very confusing, especially when you use two pie charts because someone's natural inclination is going to be to compare the size of the pie slices. And you can't do that.

So if you find yourself in a situation where it's necessary to use one of these two charts, I strongly recommend using the bar of pie chart instead of the pie of pie chart.

But I honestly wouldn't use either one if you can avoid it. (The best charts can be read without explanation and I'm not sure that would be true for either of these options for your average user.)

Scatter Charts

Scatter charts (or scatter plots) are the second option on the bottom row of the chart types.

Scatter charts plot the value of variable A given a value for variable B. For example, if I were trying to figure out if gravity is a constant, I might plot how long it takes for a ball to reach the ground when I drop it from varying heights. So I'd plot time vs. distance. From that I could eventually see that the results form a pattern which does indicate a constant. (Thanks high school physics teacher for making physics fun.)

There are five scatter plot options. The first one is a classic scatter plot. It takes variable A and plots it against variable B, creating a standalone data point for each observation. It doesn't care what order your entries are in, because there's no attempt to connect those entries to form a pattern.

The other four scatter plot options include lines drawn through each plotted point. The two smooth line options try to draw the best curved line between points. The straight line options just connect point 1 to point 2 to point 3 using straight lines between each point. The charts with markers show each of the data points on the line, the charts without markers do not.

Excel draws the line from the first set of coordinates you provide to the second to the third, etc. This introduces a time component into your data since the order you list the data points in impacts the appearance of the line. If you have data where the order of the measurements doesn't matter and you still want to draw a line through the points (like my example of dropping a ball from varying heights where it doesn't matter which height you drop it from first), then you'll want to sort your data by one of the variables before you create your scatter plot.

Here is an example of a scatter plot and a scatter plot with a line for five measurements of the time it takes for a ball dropped from different heights to reach the ground:

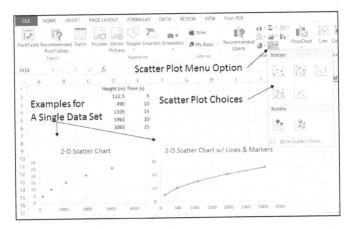

Because I sorted the data before I plotted it, we can see a nice trend line that indicates some sort of exponential relationship exists there.

You can also use scatter plots to chart more than one set of results. You just need to list the results side-by-side with the criteria you want as the horizontal axis listed first. Like this:

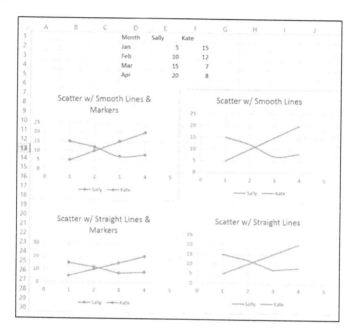

In this case we're charting the results for some measurement for two different people over the course of four months. See how the smooth line plots have lines that curve whereas the straight line plots don't? The more drastic the changes between points, the more noticeable that would become.

Note that you can also map multiple sets of data in a basic scatter plot without the lines, but including the lines makes it easier to see any difference between the data sets.

* * *

Now that you understand the basic chart types, let's talk about how to edit your charts to get them to look exactly like what you want.

CHARTS – EDITING

Chances are, once you've created a chart you'll want to edit it. With the sample charts I showed you in the last chapter I edited the name of each one, resized them, and moved them. But you can do much more than that. Like label each axis, change the legend, label your data, change the chart colors, etc.

So let's walk through some of that.

* * *

We'll start with a few fixes for if the chart doesn't seem to be working the way you expected it would.

These involve using Switch Row/Column, Select Data, and Change Chart Type in the Design tab under Chart Tools.

Switch Row/Column

Once you've created your chart you may find that the data you wanted along the bottom is along the side and the data you wanted along the side is along the bottom. The easiest way to fix this is to click on Switch Row/Column in the

Data section of the Design tab under Chart Tools. (If you can't see the Chart Tools tabs, click onto the chart somewhere and they should appear.)

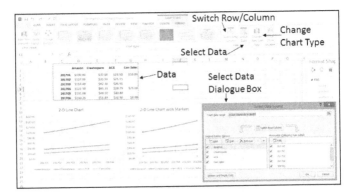

Select Data

You may also find that the data being charted isn't the data you wanted to chart. To change your data selection go to Select Data in the Design tab under Chart Tools. This will bring up the Select Data Source dialogue box. (See above.)

To remove a series of data, uncheck its box or highlight it and then click on Remove.

To add a series, click on Add, name the series, and then select the data to include from your worksheet.

To edit a series, select the series you want to edit, click on Edit, and then change the selected cells to what you want.

To change the order of the series elements, click on one of the elements and use the up and down arrows.

To remove an unwanted axis label, uncheck the box next to it.

You can also expand or reduce the data covered by a chart by clicking in the chart, going to the data table which should now be highlighted, and then left-clicking in the bottom right corner of the data, and then dragging the border of the highlighted area to either expand or contract the selection.

(If you do this, just be sure that the highlight also expands for the data labels, too. It should, but if it doesn't you'll need to do so manually.)

Change the Chart Type

If you decide that you want a bar chart instead of a column chart or a column chart instead of a line chart you can click on the chart and then go to the Insert tab and choose the new chart type.

Or you can go to the Design tab under Chart Tools, click on Change Chart Type, and choose from there.

* * *

Once you have the chart you want and the data points in the places they should be, the next step is to make sure that the chart elements you want are present. For example, that data labels are included on a pie chart or a legend is included on your bar chart.

There are two easy ways to do this using Chart Styles or Quick Layouts.

You can also easily change the color palette using Change Colors. All three are located in the Design tab under Chart Tools. (Be sure to click on your chart to see the Chart Tools.)

Choosing a Chart Style

Excel provides a number of pre-defined Chart Styles to choose from. The number of choices varies depending on the type of chart, but there are usually a variety with different colors and chart elements included or excluded.

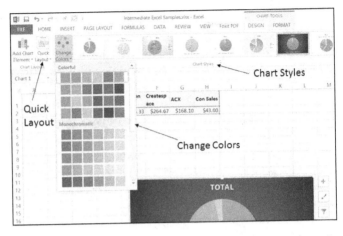

To select one, click on your chart and go to the Design tab under Chart Tools. You'll see the available options in the Chart Styles section of the tab. If there are more than seven available, you can see the rest of them by using the arrows on the right-hand side of the box.

To see what a style will look like, hold your cursor over the style image. To pick a style, click on it.

(You can choose a Chart Style and then customize it further using Chart Elements and the formatting options we'll discuss in a minute, so if you see a style that's close to what you want, pick it.)

Using a Quick Layout

The Quick Layout dropdown is also in the Design tab under Chart Tools but in the Chart Layouts section. It provides a variety of layout options to choose from. The exact number will again depend on the chart type you've chosen.

The layouts include various configurations of data labels, axis labels, legends, and grid lines. (One option for scatter charts even includes an r-squared calculation.)

To use a quick layout, click on your chart and then click on the one you want. If you hover over each one you can see what it will look like before you make your choice.

If you use a Quick Layout after you choose a Chart Style the color scheme and background colors will stay the same as the Chart Style, but the layout will update. If you choose a Quick Layout and then a Chart Style, the Chart Style will override your Quick Layout, so if you want to combine the two start with your chart style.

Using Change Colors

The easiest way to change the colors in your chart is to use one of the pre-defined color palettes available under Change Colors. Just click on Change Colors in the Design tab and then select the palette you want.

* * *

Add Chart Element

If you want more control over which chart elements are included and where they're positioned, but still want to work with pre-defined options, use the Add Chart Element dropdown menu in the Design tab.

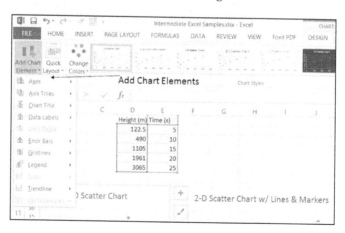

The options available will vary by chart type. For example, as you can see above, Data Table, Lines, and Up/Down Bars are not available for scatter plots.

To see the possible choices for each chart element, highlight the name and a secondary dropdown menu will appear. For each of the options shown in the secondary dropdown menu, you can hover your mouse over the option to see what it will look like before you click on it and make the change.

Let's walk through what each element represents:

1. **Axes**
   Axes allows you to add (or remove) data point labels to each axis.

2. **Axis Titles**
   Axis Titles allows you to add (or remove) a title to each axis.

3. **Chart Title**
   Chart Title allows you to either (a) remove the chart title entirely, (b) place it at the top of the chart, or (c) place it in a centered overlay position.

4. **Data Labels**
   You can use Data Labels to label each of the data points in your chart. (I find this particularly useful with pie charts, although I usually have to move the labels from their default locations, something we'll discuss how to do in the next section.)

5. **Data Table**
   Data Table allows you to add or remove a table below your chart that shows the data that was used to create the chart.

6. Error Bars

You can add bars that show the standard error, standard deviation, or percentage error in your data. (Usually you would use these if you had a data set that was predicting values and you wanted to show your potential error range. I wouldn't recommend using these on a chart unless you're dealing with data of that type and know what you're doing.)

7. Gridlines

Gridlines allows you to add (or remove) horizontal or vertical lines to your chart. These can make it easier to identify the approximate value of a specific point in the chart.

8. Legend

Legend allows you to determine the position of the legend (the listing of what each color in the chart stands for) within the chart. If you choose top and bottom, the legend elements will be in a row. If you choose right or left, they'll be displayed in a column. You can also remove the legend, although I generally wouldn't recommend that.

9. Lines

Lines allows you to add high-low lines or drop lines to a line chart.

10. Trendline

You can use Trendline to add a line onto your data to see if it fits a pattern like a linear or exponential relationship. (I'll note, though, that when I tried it on the data I purposefully constructed to follow an exponential pattern that it imposed a curve in the wrong direction.)

11. **Up/Down Bars**
    You can add Up/Down bars to a line graph. (Another one I wouldn't use unless you have a very specific reason for doing so.)

* * *

Now that you have all of the elements in place, time to discuss how to change the aesthetics of the chart. Things like size, position, and colors.

Changing the Chart Size

If you click onto a chart you've created you'll see white squares appear at each of the corners as well as in the middle of each side. Hover your mouse over each of these squares and you'll see that the cursor turns into a two sided arrow. Left-click and drag and you can increase or decrease the size of your chart. All of the elements within the chart will resize themselves automatically to fit the new size.

You can also click onto a chart and go to Size section of the Format tab under Chart Tools and specify a width and height there. Just be careful because it doesn't automatically adjust both dimensions if you just change one.

Moving a Chart

If you want to move a chart within your worksheet, left-click on an empty space within the chart, hold and drag.

(Don't click on an element within the chart, like the title, because that will just move that element around. If you do that, like I sometimes do, just Ctrl +Z to put the element back where it was and try again.)

If you want to move a chart to another worksheet or even another file (including a Word file or PowerPoint presentation), you can click onto an empty space within the chart and use Ctrl + C to copy it or Ctrl + X to cut it, and then Ctrl + V to paste it into the new location.

Moving Elements Within a Chart

You can manually move elements within a chart by left-clicking on the element and dragging it to its new location.

Renaming a Chart

To change the name of a chart, left-click on the Chart Title. You should see the title is now surrounded by a box with blue circles in each corner. You can now highlight the existing text, delete it, and then add your own text.

Renaming a Data Field as Displayed in the Legend

To change the data labels used in the legend, you need to do so in the data table that's the source of the data in the chart. As soon as you do that, the chart legend will update as well.

Changing the Color of Chart Elements

The easiest way to change the color of the chart elements is to use Change Colors, which we discussed above. If those colors aren't sufficient, you can use the Format tab under Chart Tools to change the color of each separate element in the chart one-by-one.

To do so, double-click on the element with the color you want to change, go to the Format tab under Chart Tools, and click on either the Shape Fill dropdown or the Shape Outline dropdown.

You'll use Shape Fill for bar, column, and pie graphs and Shape Outline for 2-D line graphs. (Be careful with the 3-D line graphs, because if you use Shape Outline you'll only be changing the color on the edges of the line, not the entire line.)

Once you've clicked on the dropdown for Shape Fill or Shape Outline you can use one of those provided colors or go to More Fill Colors and choose a custom color from there.

Be sure that you've only selected the elements you want to change or you may end up changing the color of all of the elements in the chart. (Something that kept happening to me when dealing with the pie charts. If that happens, just Ctrl + Z to undo and try again.)

When you click on an element, it should by default select all of the elements in the chart that relate to that variable. If it doesn't, try again rather than manually changing each one.

Another way to change the color of a chart element is to use Shape Styles in the Format tab under Chart Tools. Be sure, as above, to only select the elements you want to change. Click on the element first and then click on the style that you want.

Using the Formatting Task Pane

The box on the right-hand side of the screen that appears when you're working in a chart gives yet another way to change your formatting. (If it isn't there, double-click on the chart or an element in the chart and that should bring it up.)

The options you'll be given vary depending on the type of chart and where you've clicked within that chart. You can do things like edit the fill style for chart elements, change the chart border, specify the size of the chart, choose how the text within the chart displays, etc.

For example, with a basic pie chart this is where you'd go to expand the pie pieces outward from the center so that the pieces have separation (using pie explosion) or to rotate the pie so that the pie slice you want displayed at the top is at the top (using angle of first slice).

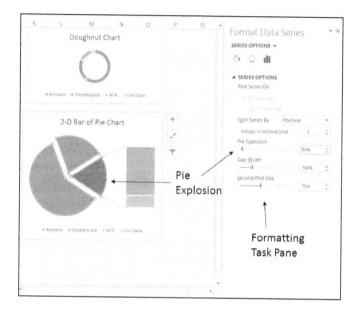

Changing Font Properties

If you want to change the font, font color, font size, or font style (italic, bold, underline), another option is to just click on the text element and then go to the Home tab and change the font options there just like you would with ordinary text in any cell.

CONCLUSION

So that was charts. They're incredibly easy to use as long as you have your data formatted in a way that makes sense for the chart type you've chosen. (I want to say that in older versions of Excel they were not as easy to use as they are now, so if you're going to use Charts a lot and they're not easy to work with in your version of Excel I'd advise upgrading.)

There are a few other chart types available in Excel. I didn't cover them because most people won't ever need them but if you have a specific type of chart you need, explore the dropdown menu choices to see if Excel provides your desired option. Chances are they will.

(Or write me and ask, I can look it up for you. I'm always happy to learn something new.)

Good luck with it. And reach out if you get stuck and need help.

APPENDIX A: BASIC TERMINOLOGY

Column

Excel uses columns and rows to display information. Columns run across the top of the worksheet and, unless you've done something funky with your settings, are identified using letters of the alphabet.

Row

Rows run down the side of the worksheet and are numbered starting at 1 and up to a very high number.

Cell

A cell is a combination of a column and row that is identified by the letter of the column it's in and the number of the row it's in. For example, Cell A1 is the cell in the first column and first row of a worksheet.

Click

If I tell you to click on something, that means to use your mouse (or trackpad) to move the arrow on the screen over to a specific location and left-click or right-click on the option. (See the next definition for the difference between left-click and right-click).

If you left-click, this selects the item. If you right-click, this generally creates a dropdown list of options to choose from. If I don't tell you which to do, left- or right-click, then left-click.

Left-click/Right-click

If you look at your mouse or your trackpad, you generally have two flat buttons to press. One is on the left side, one is on the right. If I say left-click that means to press down on the button on the left. If I say right-click that means press down on the button on the right. (If you're used to using Word or Excel you may already do this without even thinking about it. So, if that's the case then think of left-click as what you usually use to select text and right-click as what you use to see a menu of choices.)

Spreadsheet

I'll try to avoid using this term, but if I do use it, I'll mean your entire Excel file. It's a little confusing because it can sometimes also be used to mean a specific worksheet, which is why I'll try to avoid it as much as possible.

Worksheet

This is the term I'll use as much as possible. A worksheet is a combination of rows and columns that you can enter data in. When you open an Excel file, it opens to worksheet one.

Formula Bar

This is the long white bar at the top of the screen with the $f\chi$ symbol next to it.

Tab

I refer to the menu choices at the top of the screen (File, Home, Insert, Page Layout, Formulas, Data, Review, and View) as tabs. Note how they look like folder tabs from an old-time filing system when selected? That's why.

Data

I use data and information interchangeably. Whatever information you put into a worksheet is your data.

Select

If I tell you to "select" cells, that means to highlight them.

Arrow

If I say that you can "arrow" to something that just means to use the arrow keys to navigate from one cell to another.

A1:A25

If I'm going to reference a range of cells, I'll use the shorthand notation that Excel uses in its formulas. So, for example, A1:A25 will mean Cells A1 through A25. If you ever don't understand exactly what I'm referring to, you can type it into a cell in Excel using the = sign and see what cells Excel highlights. So, =A1:A25 should highlight cells A1 through A25 and =A1:B25 should highlight the cells in columns A and B and rows 1 through 25.

With Formulas Visible

Normally Excel doesn't show you the formula in a cell unless you click on that cell and then you only see the formula in the formula bar. But to help you see what I'm referring to, some of the screenshots in this guide will be provided with formulas visible. All this means is that I clicked on Show Formulas on the Formulas tab so that you could see what cells have formulas in them and what those formulas are.

Unless you do the same, your worksheet will not look like that. That's okay. Because you don't need to have your formulas visible unless you're troubleshooting something that isn't working.

Dialogue Box

I will sometimes reference a dialogue box. These are the boxes that occasionally pop up with additional options for you to choose from for that particular task. Usually I include a screen shot so you know what it should look like.

Paste Special – Values

I will sometimes suggest that you paste special-values. What this means is to paste your data using the Values option under Paste Options (the one with 123 on the clipboard). This will paste the values from the cells you copied without also bringing over any of the formulas that created those values.

Dropdown

I will occasionally refer to a dropdown or dropdown menu. This is generally a list of potential choices that you can select from. The existence of the list is indicated by an arrow next to the first available selection. I will occasionally refer to the list of options you see when you click on a dropdown arrow as the dropdown menu.

ABOUT THE AUTHOR

M.L. Humphrey is a former stockbroker with a degree in Economics from Stanford and an MBA from Wharton who has spent close to twenty years as a regulator and consultant in the financial services industry.

You can reach M.L. at mlhumphreywriter@gmail.com or at mlhumphrey.com.

CPSIA information can be obtained
at www.ICGtesting.com
Printed in the USA
LVHW041234200919
631694LV00020B/305